THE LIFE INSURANCE
DILEMMA

BY PATRICK KELLY

© 2017 Patrick Kelly

All rights reserved. No part of this book may be reproduced or transmitted in any form or by any means, electronic or mechanical, including photocopying or recording, or by any information storage and retrieval system without permission of the copyright holder.

Cover and Interior Design by Impact Partnership

ISBN 978-0-9833615-5-8

Printed in the USA

TABLE OF CONTENTS

6   **PREFACE**

10   **CHAPTER 1**
THE DIFFERENCE BETWEEN *COST* AND *NET COST*

14   **CHAPTER 2**
THE DIFFERENCE BETWEEN RENTING AND BUYING

20   **CHAPTER 3**
THE REAL COST OF TERM INSURANCE

28   **CHAPTER 4**
THE REAL COST OF PERMANENT INSURANCE

36   **CHAPTER 5**
WHAT'S RIGHT FOR YOU?

41   **IMPORTANT DISCLOSURE**

43   **ABOUT THE AUTHOR**

PREFACE

PREFACE

I've been in the life insurance industry for 25 years, and during that time I've watched fads, trends, and products come and go. Every new decade boasts the newest and the greatest, only to be superseded by the next decade's offerings. But one thing that has remained constant in all these years has been the perennial question, "Should I buy term life insurance or should I buy permanent life insurance?"

It's likely a question you've asked yourself, or one that's been asked of you. But if you're like many individuals, a clear answer has eluded you.

My goal in these next five chapters is to bring clarity to that dilemma and help make the choice simple and easy — to give you the uncluttered facts about both choices so you can make the right selection *for you* and find added peace in knowing you're walking the best path for *your* financial future.

The truth is that both types of life insurance are good options. And from a macro perspective, there isn't a "right" or "wrong" choice. However, there is a "right" or "best" answer *for you*, an answer that depends on your time horizon, your financial objectives, your risk tolerance, your budget, and your desires. Both serve significant and meaningful purposes, but each was designed to fit different needs.

It is my hope that these next few pages will cut out the noise and clutter so you can ask the right questions without sales pressure and comfortably settle on the plan that will serve your situation best and provide the security and longevity for your family that you desire.

I can give you facts and figures and data, but only *you* can choose the correct type of life insurance for your specific needs. And *that's* what is most critical. Whatever you choose, it must be right *for you*, because the only good life insurance is life insurance that's in force when you need it. And if you make the wrong choice, you might find that your *policy* expires before *you* do — and that wouldn't be good.

PREFACE

So if you own life insurance of any variety (or are considering purchasing it) this little book was written for you — to bring added peace, clarity, and understanding to your decision and to ensure the direction you choose is in perfect sync with your goals and aspirations.

THE DIFFERENCE BETWEEN *COST* AND *NET COST*

THE DIFFERENCE BETWEEN *COST* AND *NET COST*

In our society people often look at the cost (price) of an item instead of focusing on the *net cost* (value). What's the difference? A lot!

Let's first look at a simple, inexpensive household example — the light bulb. In this example, *Light Bulb A* provides 1,000 hours of light and costs $1, while *Light Bulb B* provides 4,000 hours of light and costs $2.

If a person wanted to make a buying decision based solely on cost and wanted the cheapest light bulb, which one would he choose? *Light Bulb A*, of course, because it costs only $1.

However, if that person looked beyond the *cost* of the item to the more meaningful *net cost*, he would certainly choose *Light Bulb B*. Why? Because Light Bulb B provides twice the value of *Light Bulb A*. While *Light Bulb A* provides 1,000 hours of light per $1, *Light Bulb B* provides 2,000 hours per $1 — twice as many hours. While the *cost* of *Light Bulb B* is twice as much ($2 instead of $1), the *net cost* is actually half as much (50 cents per 1,000 hours instead of $1).

You might be thinking: "That's pretty simple. Who wouldn't buy *Light Bulb B?* It's clearly the better deal."

But let me ask you: Do *you* always buy the item with the best value? Or do you sometimes fall prey to the sticker-price trap as well? That's an easy answer. You do. We all do. No one is immune. And the higher the price of an item, the more likely we shop on *cost* (price) instead of *net cost* (value).

Let's look at a different example, one that will be more pertinent to our future discussion.

Pretend you're shopping for a plane ticket to Europe. You go online and plug in the necessary information, and the computer spits out 50 different flight options. Let's assume the least expensive ticket is $500 and the most expensive is $2,000 — four times as much. Let's also assume that everything about these two flights is exactly the same. Same airline. Same flight duration. Same meals, services, and accommodations. Both flights are non-stop. Everything is absolutely identical.

CHAPTER 1

Which flight would you pick? The $500 one, of course! That's a no-brainer. Why would you spend four times more for something identical? You wouldn't. Or, at least, you *shouldn't*.

But let's add one little twist to this scenario. Let's assume that everything above, including price, stays exactly the same. The cheapest ticket is still $500 and the most expensive is still $2,000. However, what if at the bottom of the $2,000 ticket, in the "fine print," were these words: *When you step off the plane in Europe, your entire purchase price of $2,000 will be refunded to you.*

Now which ticket would you buy? The $2,000 one, of course! Why? Because while the *cost* (price) of the ticket is $2,000 — four times as much — the *net cost is $0* since your entire purchase price will be refunded to you at the end of your journey.

Do you now recognize the important difference between *cost* and *net cost*? It can be tremendous — and costly — if the right option isn't selected. So before we dig into some specifics for each of these two types of insurance, I'd like to further explore this idea of *cost* and *net cost* using a decades-old analogy: a comparison of these two types of insurance to the difference between renting a home and buying a home. And please note, this analogy, like many analogies, is only a loose comparison for the sake of illustration. It is not an identical comparison, nor is it intended to be. However, just like the airline ticket example, I think you'll find some interesting similarities.

THE DIFFERENCE BETWEEN RENTING AND BUYING

THE DIFFERENCE BETWEEN RENTING AND BUYING

For this analogy, let's pretend two individuals are looking to move into the same neighborhood. The houses they've chosen are identical homes built side by side, both valued at $250,000. The first individual, Mary, is looking to buy her home. The second individual, Peter, plans to rent.

Mary finds she can acquire a 30-year mortgage with a 5.5 percent fixed-interest rate that will cost her $1,420 per month (principal and interest) for 360 months. Peter, however, prefers to forego the higher monthly payments and move into the identical, neighboring house for only $1,000 per month — a $420 monthly savings. Peter is proud of his financial decision.

However, what Peter doesn't realize is that, over time, his rent payments are going to go up ... and up ... and up ... and UP. Even at a nominal 3.5 percent inflation rate, Peter's $420 monthly savings will evaporate in the 12th year, at which point he'll begin paying *more* each month than Mary, even though Mary is buying her home and Peter is renting. And as bad as that seems, it only gets worse from there for Peter.

In the 30th year, using the same 3.5 percent inflation rate, Peter will be paying $2,711.88 per month — almost triple the amount from where he began. See Figure 2.1 for Peter's rent payment schedule.

Monthly Rent Year 1	$1,000.00
Monthly Rent Year 2	$1,035.00
Monthly Rent Year 3	$1,071.23
Monthly Rent Year 4	$1,108.72
Monthly Rent Year 5	$1,147.52
Monthly Rent Year 6	$1,187.69
Monthly Rent Year 7	$1,229.26
Monthly Rent Year 8	$1,272.28
Monthly Rent Year 9	$1,316.81
Monthly Rent Year 10	$1,362.90

Monthly Rent Year 11	$1,410.60
Monthly Rent Year 12	$1,459.97
Monthly Rent Year 13	$1,511.07
Monthly Rent Year 14	$1,563.96
Monthly Rent Year 15	$1,618.69
Monthly Rent Year 16	$1,675.35
Monthly Rent Year 17	$1,733.99
Monthly Rent Year 18	$1,794.68
Monthly Rent Year 19	$1,857.49
Monthly Rent Year 20	$1,922.50
Monthly Rent Year 21	$1,989.79
Monthly Rent Year 22	$2,059.43
Monthly Rent Year 23	$2,131.51
Monthly Rent Year 24	$2,206.11
Monthly Rent Year 25	$2,283.33
Monthly Rent Year 26	$2,363.24
Monthly Rent Year 27	$2,445.96
Monthly Rent Year 28	$2,531.57
Monthly Rent Year 29	$2,620.17
Monthly Rent Year 30	$2,711.88

Figure 2.1

Mary's monthly payment, on the other hand (as it relates to principal and interest), has remained at $1,420 over that entire 30-year period — ending exactly where it began — which is good news for Mary. But that's just a snapshot of her monthly payment. The news gets even brighter for Mary (or worse for Peter, depending on one's perspective) as we look at the *total* financial picture over that 30-year period.

Since Mary's monthly payment (principal and interest) has stayed level at $1,420, she will have paid $511,200, not including maintenance, taxes, insurance, and repairs, to purchase her house over the 30-year-mortgage period. Peter, on the other hand, beginning with a rental amount of $1,000 per month and an inflation rate of just 3.5 percent, will have paid a whopping $619,472 during that same timeframe — $108,282 *more* than Mary, who actually purchased her home. See Figure 2.2.

	Mary's Annual Mortgage Payment*	Peter's Annual Rent Payment
Year 1	$17,040	$12,000
Year 2	$17,040	$12,420
Year 3	$17,040	$12,855
Year 4	$17,040	$13,305
Year 5	$17,040	$13,770
Year 6	$17,040	$14,252
Year 7	$17,040	$14,751
Year 8	$17,040	$15,267
Year 9	$17,040	$15,802
Year 10	$17,040	$16,355
Year 11	$17,040	$16,927
Year 12	$17,040	$17,520
Year 13	$17,040	$18,133
Year 14	$17,040	$18,767
Year 15	$17,040	$19,424
Year 16	$17,040	$20,104
Year 17	$17,040	$20,808
Year 18	$17,040	$21,536
Year 19	$17,040	$22,290
Year 20	$17,040	$23,070
Year 21	$17,040	$23,877
Year 22	$17,040	$24,713
Year 23	$17,040	$25,578
Year 24	$17,040	$26,473
Year 25	$17,040	$27,400

	Mary's Annual Mortgage Payment*	Peter's Annual Rent Payment
Year 26	$17,040	$28,359
Year 27	$17,040	$29,352
Year 28	$17,040	$30,379
Year 29	$17,040	$31,442
Year 30	$17,040	$32,543
30-Year Total	**$511,200**	**$619,472**

Figure 2.2

*Principal and interest only

Now how smart does Peter feel about his initial decision to save $420 a month?

And let's not forget, this is just looking at things from the out-of-pocket mortgage *payment* standpoint. It doesn't yet reflect the most significant difference between these two individuals' financial statuses at the end of 30 years — equity! This one is a real game-changer.

Even though Mary has paid $511,200 for her home during that 30-year period (principal and interest), if we factor in the same 3.5 percent inflation rate, we realize her home would now be worth $701,698! And guess what? That's *all* Mary's money. Since her loan has been fulfilled by her 30 years of payments, all of this equity is hers to keep if she ever decides to sell her home, minus any selling expenses, of course.

So not only did Mary pay less from an "out-of-pocket" *payment* standpoint than Peter — $511,200 vs. $619,472 over that 30-year period — she also ended up with a significant asset to show for all of those payments: a house worth nearly three-quarters of a million dollars.

And how did Peter fare? What did he have to show for his 30 years of payments? Well, not much. As a matter of fact, nothing! Even though Peter paid $619,472 during that 30-year period, he accumulated *zero in equity*. All of his monthly payments went to grow his landlord's net worth, not his own.

Granted, we can't overlook the fact that Peter *did* receive the privilege of living in a nice house during those 30 years, which is important. However, in hindsight, it appears it might not have been one of Peter's wisest long-term financial decisions, especially since it built no financial asset he could call his own, even after spending well over half a million dollars.

So how does this story of Mary and Peter relate to our question of which life insurance option is best for you? Let's take a look.

THE REAL COST OF TERM INSURANCE

THE REAL COST OF TERM INSURANCE

Before we look at some specific details of term insurance, there is one vital question you *must* answer in order to ultimately make the correct choice between these two different life insurance options. The question is this: *"How long do you want your life insurance to stay in force?"*

Really. How long? Don't make that a rhetorical question. Pause for a moment and ask yourself that very thing. Is it five years? Thirty years? Until you die?

There's not just one right answer. Any can be correct. However, there *is* likely only one correct answer *for you*. So take a moment, jot down that answer, and we'll come back to it once we've finished the next couple of chapters. The answer to this question will likely be *the* central tenant upon which you base your eventual choice.

In its simplest form, every life insurance policy (and I mean *every* policy) fits into one of two simple categories: term life insurance or permanent life insurance. While there are many different and confusing names for each, such as 10-year term, 20-year term, mortgage life, universal life, whole life, indexed universal life, and so on, every type of policy I have ever seen is really just some form of one of these two types of insurance.

Term life insurance might represent the purest form of insurance I know. It is simply this: an individual pays a premium, and when the insured dies, assuming the policy is still in force, someone receives a death benefit. That's it!

And while it is simple to understand how this type of insurance works, the long-term, financial ramifications of choosing this option are not always as readily apparent, just as the full ramifications of Peter's decision to rent weren't completely obvious to him at the time he signed the lease.

In my opinion, there are four characteristics that term insurance shares with renting a home. These are:

Similarity No. 1 — Lower cost (premium) initially
Similarity No. 2 — No equity (cash value)
Similarity No. 3 — Cost (premium) goes up

CHAPTER 3

Similarity No. 4 — Contract (coverage) ends

So let's take a look at these four characteristics as they relate to this simplest form of insurance. Figure 3.1 is a generic illustration for a hypothetically insured person in good health utilizing a common type of life insurance known as 10-year term insurance.

10-Year Level Premium Term Insurance — Age 35*
(Hypothetical Illustration)

End of Year	End of Year Age	Premium	Death Benefit
1	36	$294	$350,000
2	37	$294	$350,000
3	38	$294	$350,000
4	39	$294	$350,000
5	40	$294	$350,000
		$1,470	
6	41	$294	$350,000
7	42	$294	$350,000
8	43	$294	$350,000
9	44	$294	$350,000
10	45	$294	$350,000
		$2,940	
11	46	$1,701	$350,000
12	47	$1,855	$350,000
13	48	$2,023	$350,000
14	49	$2,210	$350,000
15	50	$2,384	$350,000
		$13,113	
16	51	$2,526	$350,000
17	52	$2,816	$350,000
18	53	$3,066	$350,000
19	54	$3,426	$350,000
20	55	$3,876	$350,000
		$28,823	

Figure 3.1

As you can see in this illustration in Figure 3.1, the cost each year for $350,000 of term life insurance for a 35-year-old individual is just $294 for the first 10 years. That means that over its entire 10-year policy term, this owner would only pay $3,000 to provide a $350,000 life insurance benefit for his beneficiary. So as I outlined in Similarity No. 1, that is quite inexpensive — *initially*. Just $294 per year to make sure someone he loves, or someone he owes, gets paid $350,000 if he dies during that 10-year period.

But how much cash value (think home equity) has been built during this period? See Figure 3.2.

Term Insurance after 10 years
(Hypothetical Example)

Cost: $2,940
Cash Value: $0
Net Cost: $2,940
Death Benefit: $350,000

Figure 3.2

That's right! Zero. As I mentioned in Similarity No. 2, there is no cash value built up over this time period. All of the premium has been dedicated to purchasing the death benefit, keeping the policy in force. That's not a bad thing. It's just, as you will soon see, important to consider as you are evaluating the **net cost** of term life insurance.

Again, going back to our analogy, if you rented a house for 10 years and then decided to move out, how much of those rental payments would your landlord give back to you when you left?

That's right! None!

The same is true with term insurance. It provides a death benefit as long as the proper premium is paid, but once the premium ceases, the coverage ends, and there is generally no return of all those years of premium payments to the owner. As is the case with most things, exceptions do exist, so it's important to point out that this example refers to a standard, traditional type of term insurance.

While term life insurance is inexpensive initially, here's where understanding what you're buying becomes critical. An individual

CHAPTER 3

is usually allowed to keep his 10-year term policy *beyond* the 10-year term period; however, he would rarely, if ever, choose to do so because, beginning in year 11, the policy usually becomes a lot more expensive. (See Figure 3.1, Year 11 and following, for an example.)

As you can see, it can get quite expensive!

So what typically happens at this point if the insured person wants to continue his policy past the 10-year mark? Assuming the individual is healthy and can still qualify for life insurance at a good rate, he would likely apply for a *new* 10-year term policy at his current age instead of continuing the policy he purchased 10 years ago and paying the new, astronomical rate (refer again to Figure 3.1). This would allow him to obtain a premium much lower than if he simply continued his original policy. Compare the total premium paid in years 11–20 in Figure 3.1 ($25,883) to the same 10-year period if the insured requalified as in Figure 3.3 ($5,250). In this example, by requalifying at a preferred rate instead of simply continuing his original policy, the insured would have saved $20,633, or roughly 80 percent, by reapplying for a new 10-year term policy and receiving a preferred rating like he received when he was 35 years old.

10-Year Level Premium Term Insurance — Age 45*
(Hypothetical Illustration)

End of Year	End of Year Age	Premium	Death Benefit
1	46	$525	$350,000
2	47	$525	$350,000
3	48	$525	$350,000
4	49	$525	$350,000
5	50	$525	$350,000
		$2,625	
6	51	$525	$350,000
7	52	$525	$350,000
8	53	$525	$350,000
9	54	$525	$350,000
10	55	$525	$350,000
		$5,250	

THE REAL COST OF TERM INSURANCE

11	56	$3,720	$350,000
12	57	$4,148	$350,000
13	58	$4,625	$350,000
14	59	$5,157	$350,000
15	60	$5,750	$350,000
		$28,649	
16	61	$6,411	$350,000
17	62	$7,148	$350,000
18	63	$7,970	$350,000
19	64	$8,887	$350,000
20	65	$9,909	$350,000
		$68,974	

Figure 3.3

And if an individual wanted to keep life insurance throughout his entire lifetime, this cycle of purchasing a new policy every 10 years (or whatever the term period happened to be) would repeat itself over and over and over again. And this is where Similarity No. 3 — cost goes up — enters the picture. See Figure 3.4 (Hypothetical Example).

	TERM
10 yrs (age 45 yrs)	Total Cost: $2,940 Equity: 0 Net Cost: $2,940 Coverage: $350,000
20 yrs (age 55 yrs)	Total Cost: $8,820 Equity: 0 Net Cost: $8,820 Coverage: $350,000
30 yrs (age 65 yrs)	Total Cost: $23,940 Equity: 0 Net Cost: $23,940 Coverage: $350,000
40 yrs (age 75 yrs)	Total Cost: $93,220 Equity: 0 Net Cost: $93,220 Coverage: $350,000
50 yrs (age 85 yrs)	Total Cost: $256,160 Equity: 0 Net Cost: $256,160 Coverage: 0

Figure 3.4

Let's take a look at Figure 3.4 in detail to define what these different terms mean and how this would play out over the course of 50 years.

In this hypothetical example, the cost for $350,000 of life insurance for 10 years beginning at age 35 is $294 per year. Assuming the policyholder re-applied every ten years and *did* recieve preferred rates, at age 45 it increases to $525 per year, taking the 20-year total premium paid to $8,820. At age 55 it rises to $1,512 per year, bringing the 30-year total to $23,940. At age 65 the cost goes up again, but quite significantly this time, to $6,928 per year, bringing the 40-year total to $93,220.

Can you see the pattern here? The older you get, the more expensive life insurance becomes. And at age 75, no longer assuming the insured is healthy enough to requalify for a preferred rate but rather a standard rate, the cost increases precipitously to $16,294 per year — 5,542 percent *more expensive* than when the individual first purchased his term insurance. So in this hypothetical example, during this 50-year time period, the individual would have paid a whopping total of $256,160 in premiums.

Before we continue, and it's important we do, let's pause for a moment and go back to review Similarity No. 2 — no cash value. If an individual followed this path, he would have paid $256,160 in premium to obtain $350,000 of life insurance coverage over a 50-year period. And how much cash value did he accumulate during this time period?

Again, if you answered zero, you'd be correct.

In this hypothetical example, since there is no cash value that has accumulated inside of the term life insurance policy, both the **cost** and the **net cost** of the policy over that 50-year period from age 35 to age 85 is the same – $256,160. In other words, this individual paid 73 percent ($256,160 / $350,000) of the death benefit amount in premium during that 50-year period, yet has no accumulated cash value.

Please understand, I believe term insurance is a good deal, especially in the early years for the family whose breadwinner dies during that time period. And if that's the only insurance a family can afford, then it is my *strong* belief that's *exactly* what they should purchase, because, as I originally said, the only good life insurance is life insurance that's in force at the time of the insured's death.

But now enters the real problem: Similarity No. 4 — coverage ends.

In this hypothetical example (Figure 3.4), even if an insured wanted to continue his life insurance beyond age 85, he generally could not. Most companies in the industry usually don't allow it. At some point in the future, whether at age 85 or some other age, even if all premiums have been paid, the insured generally can no longer keep his policy. And that can be a tragedy if he still needs it.

But this is where permanent life insurance enters the picture. It *is* designed to last for a person's entire lifetime, regardless of what age is reached. And not only that, it also has three other unique characteristics that can be meaningful to the insured as well. Let's take a look.

This illustration is purely hypothetical and is not intended to represent any particular company or product. Any similarity between this product and any others in the marketplace is purely coincidental.

THE REAL COST OF PERMANENT INSURANCE

THE REAL COST OF PERMANENT INSURANCE

Just as term insurance has four similarities to renting a home, permanent insurance has four similarities to buying a home. They are:

Similarity No. 1 — Higher cost (premium) initially
Similarity No. 2 — Can build equity (cash value)
Similarity No. 3 — Designed to be level cost (premium)
Similarity No. 4 — Contract (coverage) designed to last a person's entire life

To illustrate these four similarities, just as we did for term insurance in Chapter 3, let's look at a hypothetical summary of what a permanent life insurance policy might look like in 10-year increments. (See Figure 4.1.*) Please understand that the numbers and terminology in this chart won't make complete sense to you at this point, but they will by the end of this chapter.

	PERMANENT
10 yrs (age 45 yrs)	Total Cost: $36,000 Equity: $35,879 Net Cost: $121 Coverage: $385,879 Net Cost Advantage: +$2,819
20 yrs (age 55 yrs)	Total Cost: $72,000 Equity: $91,243 Net Cost: (-19,243) Coverage: $441,243 Net Cost Advantage: +$28,063
30 yrs (age 65 yrs)	Total Cost: $108,000 Equity: $170,079 Net Cost: (-62,079) Coverage: $520,079 Net Cost Advantage: +$86,019
40 yrs (age 75 yrs)	Total Cost: $144,000 Equity: $254,602 Net Cost: (-110,602) Coverage: $604,602 Net Cost Advantage: +$203,822
50 yrs (age 85 yrs)	Total Cost: $180,000 Equity: $256,032 Net Cost: (-76,032) Coverage: $606,032 Net Cost Advantage: +$332,192

Figure 4.1

THE LIFE INSURANCE DILEMMA

As you can see, over a 10-year period an individual purchasing this type of policy would pay $36,000 in total premium ($250 per month for 10 years) compared to just $2,940 for term insurance. This presents us with Similarity No. 1 between permanent life insurance and buying a home: the initial cost can be more expensive than the alternative. And as you can see from this example, it can sometimes be a significant difference — *initially.*

But that only represents the cost of each policy and not the *net cost.* Let's bring that into the discussion and see how the picture changes. See Figure 4.2.

Permanent Insurance after 10 years*
(Hypothetical Example)

Total 10-year Cost:	$36,000
Cash Value:	$35,879
Net Cost:	**$121**
Death Benefit:	$385,879
Net Cost Advantage:	**+$2,819**

Figure 4.2

In this hypothetical example, the *cost* of permanent insurance over a 10-year period is $36,000. However, unlike term insurance, much of that premium goes to build the cash value and is not just allocated to pay for the death benefit and other expenses. This allows the cash value during this 10-year timeframe to grow to a sizeable $35,879 — just $121 short of what the policy owner actually paid into the policy!

What this means is that if the individual canceled his policy after 10 years, he would receive a check for $35,879, making the *net cost* only $121. Wow! Does that remind you of stepping off the plane in Europe and receiving a refund for your $2,000 ticket purchase? It should. It's quite similar even though it takes place over a much longer period of time.

Now which policy is less expensive? Based on *cost*, it's still the term life insurance, but if we evaluate it on *net cost*, the permanent insurance is less expensive — a lot less expensive — $2,819 less expensive to be exact.

$2,940 (*total net cost of term*) - $121 (*total net cost of permanent*)
= $2,819

Figure 4.3

I like to call that the **net cost advantage**. This is simply how much cheaper it is to purchase one policy over another, based on *net cost*.

Similarity No. 2 between permanent insurance and buying a home is the fact that both, under normal circumstances, are designed to create equity (cash value) for the owner. And as you can see, even after just 10 years that cash value can be quite significant. But just like Mary's house purchase, the more time that passes, the more compelling this becomes. Let's keep walking through the decades. See Figure 4.4.

Permanent Insurance after 20 years*
(Hypothetical Example)

Total 20-year Cost:	$72,000
Cash Value:	$91,243
Net Cost:	- $19,243
Death Benefit:	$441,243
Net Cost Advantage:	+$28,063

Figure 4.4

Do you notice how the net cost in year 20 is negative? Do you know what a *negative net cost* means? It is the same thing as a *profit*, which is the terminology we will use from here forward. It means a person would get back that much *more* than he put in. In other words, a *net cost* of negative $19,243 is the same thing as a $19,243 *profit*.

As you look at the total cost of this permanent policy over the entire 20-year period, you may or may not notice that the premium remained level. It didn't go up. The first 10-year period cost $36,000 in total premium, as did the second 10 years, bringing the total 20-year premium amount to $72,000. That's Similarity No. 3. The premium, just like the cost of a 30-year mortgage (principal and interest), is designed to remain level.

So while the term policy increased from $294 per year in years 1–10 to $588 per year in years 11–20, the permanent policy's premium remained exactly the same.

And what about the cash value? Did you notice how it grew in this example? It grew to $91,243 after 20 years, making the *net cost* a negative $19,243. In other words, after 20 years, this insured could cancel his policy and get back $19,243 **more** than he put into it over that same period of time, so the **net cost advantage** in the permanent policy's favor has become $28,063. Not too shabby.

$8,820 (20-year *total net cost of term*) − (−$19,243) (20-year *total net cost of permanent*) = $28,063

Another way to calculate this is:

$8,820 (20-year *total net cost of term*) + $19,243 (20-year *profit of permanent*) = $28,063

Figure 4.5

But let's keep going, because it only gets better, at least for the policy owner in this hypothetical example. See Figure 4.6.

Permanent Insurance after 30 years*
(Hypothetical Example)

Total 30-year Cost:	$108,000
Cash Value:	$170,079
Profit:	**$62,079**
Death Benefit:	$520,079
Net Cost Advantage:	**+$86,019**

Figure 4.6

THE REAL COST OF PERMANENT INSURANCE

For years 21–30, the annual premium again stays level at $3,600, bringing the 30-year total premium to $108,000. The cash value has risen to $170,079, making the profit $62,079. And the net cost advantage has blossomed to $86,019.

Now let's look at Figure 4.7 and see what this policy could potentially look like after 40 years.

Permanent Insurance after 40 years*
(Hypothetical Example)

Total 40-year Cost:	$144,000
Cash Value:	$254,602
Profit:	**$110,602**
Death Benefit:	$604,602
Net Cost Advantage:	**+$203,822**

Figure 4.7

As mentioned previously, the longer this comparison runs, the more compelling the permanent insurance becomes, as you can see in the numbers above. It's after the first 40 years, though, that I want to pause and point out, once again, the importance of this *net cost advantage*. What the *net cost advantage* represents is how much "cheaper" (from a net cost perspective) it has been to buy permanent insurance versus term insurance over a certain period of time, just as the $2000 plane ticket was "cheaper" than the $500 ticket because those who purchased the $2,000 ticket received their entire $2,000 back when they stepped off the plane. And as you can see in Figure 4.7, the permanent life insurance in this hypothetical example has a *net cost advantage* of more than $200,000.

You may be asking yourself, "How is the *net cost advantage* calculated?" It's quite simple. It's the combination of the *net cost* of term insurance after 40 years ($93,220) that the insured would have had to spend if he had purchased term insurance, but didn't have to spend because he bought permanent, added to the $110,602 *profit* from the permanent insurance that he did receive. When you add those two numbers together you get the **net cost advantage** which, in this case, is a whopping $203,822. In other words, the *net cost* of the permanent insurance is actually $203,822 "cheaper" than the net cost of the term insurance over this 40-year timeframe.

And as significant as that is, it's only after the next 10-year period in this example that we experience what I believe to be the most critical characteristic of permanent life insurance: Similarity No. 4 between buying a home and buying permanent life insurance — the fact that coverage is designed to last a person's entire lifetime, assuming proper premiums are paid.

Permanent Insurance after 50 years*
(Hypothetical Example)

Total 50-year Cost:	$180,000
Cash Value:	$256,032
Profit:	**$76,032**
Death Benefit:	$606,032
Net Cost Advantage:	*+$332,192*

Figure 4.8

Do you remember what happened to the term policy in Chapter 3 when the insured reached age 85? That's right! It ended. The death benefit disappeared because the insured reached an age at which the company no longer allowed him to buy term insurance. He became too old, which means the insured paid all those decades of premium and ended with nothing to show for it, not even a death benefit.

Think how disappointing that would be for someone who wanted to continue his life insurance until he needed it. And when is that? When he dies. It's kind of like a renter being told by his landlord he can no longer live in the house he'd rented for 50 years because the owner decided to sell it or move back into it, leaving him without a place to live. Luckily for the renter, though, this is generally a temporary problem, as most individuals can find a new place to live. Unfortunately, for the term life insurance owner, it's not so simple. He no longer has that choice. His term insurance is gone, and he generally does not have the option to purchase it again.

THE REAL COST OF PERMANENT INSURANCE

One important side note in this discussion, however, is to point out that most term insurance policies become so expensive in the later years that most individuals let their policies lapse long before the point at which they are no longer allowed to buy a policy anyway. But in either case, the insured finds himself without the important insurance he's spent so much money on throughout the years.

And this, in my opinion, is the chief benefit of permanent life insurance. There is not some arbitrary age at which the issuing company says an insured can no longer keep his policy. It's his for as long as he lives, as long as the proper premiums are paid.

And before we move on to the last chapter, did you notice the tremendous growth of the death benefit during that 50-year period? Amazing!

This illustration is purely hypothetical and is not intended to represent any particular company or product. Any similarity between this product and any others in the marketplace is purely coincidental.

WHAT'S RIGHT FOR YOU?

WHAT'S RIGHT FOR YOU?

Now let's bring the discussion back to what's most important — *YOU!* As with most things in life, there isn't just one correct answer for all people, especially when choosing between two good options. (And make no mistake, these are both good options.) The real challenge *isn't* trying to decide which policy is best but, rather, which policy is best for *you*.

The answer to this question will vary from person to person, but likely the most significant contributing factor is the answer to the question at the beginning of Chapter 3: "How long do you want your life insurance to stay in force?" This will be a primary and driving force in your decision.

So what did you write down for an answer? Do you want your life insurance to stay in force for five years? 20 years? Your entire lifetime?

Your answer to that question leads us to the next question: "How does that timeframe help you decide which policy is the best fit?" The easiest way to walk you through that is to give you a visual road map to help you sort out that nagging question. And once you walk through this incredibly simple chart, I think you'll see it's not a very complicated decision.

Follow the flow chart below to answer this question:

How long do you want your life insurance to stay in force?

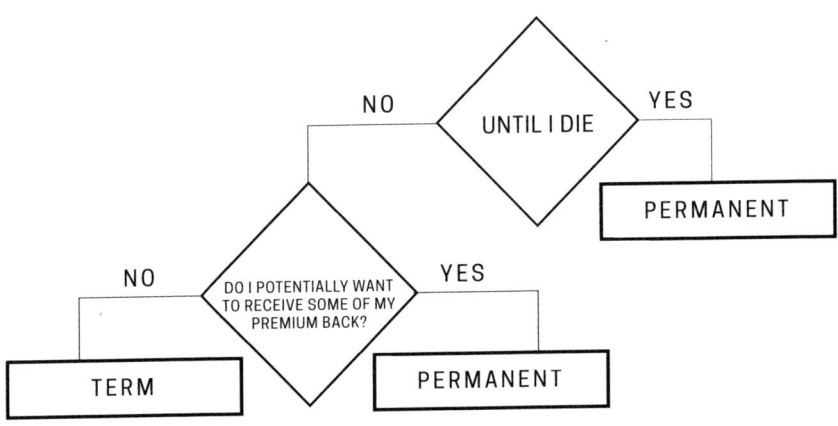

Figure 5.1

As you can see in Figure 5.1, there are two important questions you need to answer to help determine the option that best suits your needs. Those questions are:

1. How long do I want my life insurance to stay in force?

2. Do I want to receive some or all of my premium back if I cancel the policy or die?

This flow chart definitely makes some vast generalizations, but its goal is simply to help point you in the direction that may be most appropriate for your specific desires. However, it does not ask the critical and pragmatic question, "How much can your budget afford?"

The reason this is such a critical question is because if your budget can't accommodate your entire life insurance need being met through permanent insurance, regardless of your answers to the previous questions above, then term insurance, by default, will likely be your best bet — at least partially. But here's the twist.

There's a third option most individuals don't consider. A remarkably compelling option. That option is to purchase some of both types of insurance. That's the good news with life insurance. It doesn't have to be an "all or nothing" decision. You don't have to make a choice between buying all term insurance or all permanent insurance. You can buy a little bit of each and get the best of both worlds — a policy that builds cash value for your future and one that allows you to buy an amount of coverage large enough to meet your life insurance needs — all at a price within your monthly budget.

The other nice feature about purchasing both types of policies is that, as your income grows, you can generally convert part (or all) of your term insurance into a permanent insurance policy. And if both policies are with the same company, you can usually do this without having to go through the underwriting process again.

What could this look like in the real world? Let's say you

WHAT'S RIGHT FOR YOU?

need $750,000 in life insurance to properly protect your family. One possible option could be to purchase a $250,000 permanent insurance policy and a $500,000 term insurance policy, thereby obtaining the proper amount of death benefit at a price within your current budget. Then, every year or two as your income grows, you could convert $50,000 or $100,000 of that term insurance to your permanent policy until eventually all $750,000 is permanent insurance you can keep throughout your entire lifetime. It's sort of like being able to buy your house one room at a time.

So what's the right choice for you? Where do you go from here?

The best "next step" is to sit down with a properly licensed insurance agent who can assist you with the process of determining what best suits your specific needs, goals, and desires, and can walk you through the process of determining the proper amount of life insurance — for *you*. Then, and only then, once the numbers have been run for each type of policy, will you be able to answer those nagging, perennial questions: *Should I buy term insurance? Should I buy permanent insurance? Or should I buy a little of both?*

IMPORTANT DISCLOSURE

The views, opinions, and hypothetical examples in this publication are not meant to provide specific financial, insurance, or investment advice. Please consult with a trained and licensed financial professional to discuss your unique risk tolerance, time horizons, financial objectives, and retirement goals.

ABOUT THE AUTHOR

Patrick Kelly is the author of five national best-selling books, *Tax-Free Retirement* (2007), *The Retirement Miracle* (2011), *Stress-Free Retirement* (2013), *The 5 Retirement Myths* (2015), and *Seven Secrets to a Happy Retirement* (2016), which together have sold more than 1.5 million copies. Patrick's "client first" philosophy is the centerpiece of all his messages.